LIFE

Living in faithfulness and encouragement

Nadine Gamble

WESTBOW
P R E S S®
A DIVISION OF THOMAS NELSON
& ZONDERVAN

WestBow Press books may be ordered through booksellers or by contacting:

WestBow Press
A Division of Thomas Nelson & Zondervan
1663 Liberty Drive
Bloomington, IN 47403
www.westbowpress.com
844-714-3454

ISBN: 979-8-3850-4289-0 (sc)
ISBN: 979-8-3850-4288-3 (e)

Library of Congress Control Number: 2025901268

Print information available on the last page.

WestBow Press rev. date: 03/06/2025

DEDICATION

This book is dedicated to my natural and spiritual family – my seven children who assisted with some of the ideas for this book and for the encouraging words and prayers prayed for me on this part of my journey. Thank you for believing that I could do what looked and seemed impossible. A very special thank you to the Tyson family who were instrumental in my spiritual journey, as I fulfill my kingdom assignment. To my Pastor James E. Tyson II – thank you for allowing God to use you to inspire me to write this book. Many times, Pastor spoke in his teachings saying, "there are books in you". At the time, I never focused too much on what Pastor said, because I had always concluded that word was not for me but was for the brilliant minded young people. However, when my pastor challenged me with the question, "What are you believing God for that seems like an impossibility?" – I responded in the comments, "Possibly write a book"! I don't think I was serious about writing a book at the time, but God had another plan. I was not aware of the prophetic words God allowed my pastor to speak to help bring forth this assignment into existence. The manifestation for what God is doing came a few months later, when I had all but forgotten what was said to me by my pastor. This time, God used my pastor to speak prophetically and declare the words God said, "write a book of poems and affirmations". That sealed it for me – no more hesitation, I know God's voice! I had to obey, even if it moved me out of my comfort zone – and it has.

As the scripture says, in Philippians 4:13 (ESV), "I can do all things through Him who strengthens me". This journey has been a faith builder for me. I thank God for revealing His word in my life through my pastor and others. The very first time I received a prophecy about writing a book, came through God's messenger, Dr. Lamont Turner, as he was speaking predictions for the year on Pastor Krista Tyson's prayer call. I had my pad and pencil in hand trying to write down the predictions. Pastor Turner spoke, and said these words, "I see you; you have a pad and pencil in your hand, you will write a book". That statement stunned me, awe and fear consumed me for a short while. I soon forgot what was said to me by Dr. Turner, two years later, I now see God bringing that prophetic word into manifestation. God be glorified! Thank you, Jesus!

CONTENTS

CONTENTS

INTRODUCTION

Do you realize you have the power to change your life circumstances? The word of God is a blueprint for how we are to maneuver and walk through this wilderness on earth called LIFE. God's word is filled with inspirations that describe who He is, what He does, and what He can and will do. We all go through pain, suffering, tragedy and disappointments at some time in our lives. It's important that we fill our minds with positive information that will encourage us, such as quotes of affirmations, words of inspiration and prayers that develop unwavering faith and perseverance that move mountains.

It's important that we feed our minds daily with information that will help us to have positive thoughts through the tough times in our lives, or the wilderness experiences. I have attempted, with the help of the Holy Spirit to align what is written in this book with what is spoken by God in His Word. I hope and pray all who read and meditate on what is said will receive something that will uplift and inspire you to push forward in-spite of any darkness, chaos or walls in your life.

Remember, only under the darkness of night can a star truly shine. May there be quotes, poems, prayers in this book that are like stars that shine and bring light into any darkness that may occur in your life.

A MIGHTY FORTRESS
IS OUR GOD

This song is said to be a song to inspire soldiers against the enemy of fear during a war, so it falls in line with what we are experiencing as soldiers in the army of the Lord. There is a war going on and this song encourages us to put our trust in the sovereign God who has all the power over any enemy that we may face. This song exalts God to a high and lofty position in the hearts and minds of those who believe the message of the song. This song is a paraphrase of Psalms 46. This song has been a frequent visitor to my mind since I began writing this book, I believe there must be some significant reason for the message it sends out.

(1)
A mighty fortress is our God
A bulwark never failing
Our helper amid the flood
Of mortal ills prevailing

For still our ancient foe
Doth seek to work us woe
His crafts and powers are great
And armed with cruel hate
On earth is not his equal

Did we in our own strength confide
Our striving would be losing
Were not the right man on our side
The man of God's own choosing
Dost ask who that may be
Christ Jesus it is He
Lord Sabaoth is His Name
From age to age the same
And he must win the battle
The word above all earthly powers

(2)
No thanks to them abideth
The spirit and gifts are ours
Through Him who with us sideth
Let good and kindred go
This mortal life also
The body they may kill
God's truth abideth still
His kingdom is forever
Author: Martin Luther 1529

THE MEANING OF LIFE

To pursue your full potential and become the best you can become in all areas of life and enjoy the journey every step of the way, even when it's painful.

Life is a special opportunity to experience grace and to have an impact for all eternity through a relationship with the Creator of all things.

Life is an opportunity to develop a relationship with God, with others, and to serve the Lord and other people.

Life is a special gift from God. God wants us to live our life for Him and to have joy and gratitude.

Life equals Survival.

One word for life: Growth.

We grow one way or another. Physically, mentally, emotionally, from the day we are born to the day we die.

LET'S PRAY (ACTS 1:3-4)

There is power in praying God's word together. We are stronger together, there is unity, there is strength.

Prayer

Lord Jesus, we pray that the good seed of the word will grow in our minds and hearts. A great faith that prevails over all evil and perseveres through dark days. Your word O Lord promises us that no weapon formed against us will prosper. Holy Spirit activate within each and every person the faith to face this day and every day called today and the entire rest of their lives. Father God may your grace be our sufficiency, in our weakness, may we be strong because you fill our cup to overflowing with your power and your presence, "Shalom" may your peace that is above all human understanding guard our hearts and minds in Christ Jesus, as you walk with us. Through the valley of the shadow, may your perfect love drive out all fear for you are with us. Your rod and your staff comfort us O Lord. May the joy of your salvation be our strength as we learn to keep our eyes on you Lord. The author and perfector of our faith. Lord Jesus Christ the Light of the World now and always. In the Almighty name of our Lord and Savior Jesus Christ, Amen.

AN ALTER OF THANKSGIVING

The twenty-four elders fell face down before the one seated on the throne and they worshipped the one who lives forever and ever, and they cast their crowns before the throne. Revelation 4:10-11 ESV

Oh, give thanks unto the Lord, "why?", because he is good. O Lord, your mercy lasts, (how long?) forever! Thank you, Lord, you are the great king above all gods.

Thank you, Jesus, you are my Savior, my Lord, my God, my friend, my justifier, my sanctifier and my satisfier. Thank you, Jesus, you are the peace that rules my mind.

Thank you, Lord Jesus, you re the joy bells that keep ringing in my soul.

Thank you, Jesus, you are the healer of all my diseases. You cause them to dry up and die by your stripes.

Thank you, Jesus, you are my midnight song, my glory and the lifter of my head. Thank you, Jesus, you are the Lilly in all my valleys.

Like a flower, you are morning dew.

Thank you, Jesus, you are my comforter, counselor and where my strength comes from.

O Lord you are my strong tower.

Thank you, Jesus, you shelter, protect and provide a safe place for me.

Thank you, Jesus, you are Alpha and Omega, the beginning and the end.

Thank you, Jesus, you are my heart's desire.

Amen.

THY KINGDOM COME
(MATTHEW 6:10)

Trust in the Lord with all your heart, and do not lean on your own understanding. In all your ways acknowledge him and he will make straight your paths. Proverbs 3:5-6 (ESV)

Heavenly Father, help us as we live to embrace your kingdom values.

O Lord, help us to set goals that will advance your kingdom agenda.

Lord Jesus, our world, our churches and our families need your kingdom agenda.

Lord Jesus, help us to assemble in unity to address the issues that deride us.

Father God, help us to follow your kingdom agenda in every area of our lives.

Help us Lord Jesus, to purpose in our hearts to pray for your kingdom and will to be done, because yours is the kingdom and the power and the glory.

Lord Jesus, help us to align ourselves underneath your hand, so we can access your full power and glory.

Thank you, Lord Jesus, that under your kingdom rule we touch heaven and change earth.

Lord Jesus, make us like you, so we can reach and equip as many people as possible for your kingdom.

In the name of Jesus Christ.

Amen.

‧‧♦♦♦♦‧‧

CHAPTER 1

ASCENSION THINKING

ASCENSION ATTENTION #1: KINGDOM MINDED

Set your mind on the things that are above not on the things that are on the earth. For you have died and your life is hidden with Christ in God. Colossians 3:2-3 ESV

We say, "we're going up-up-up!" But do we really believe what we are saying? Are we willing to do what it takes to ascend upward, or do we want to stay in our comfort zones, stuck in a rut and in the last command God gave us? Think about it; for instance, if you know you were called by God to fulfill a certain function or position that would take you to a higher calling in kingdom work, would you be willing to trust God's decision and say, "Yes, I surrender to your will" – or would you try to find every excuse as to why you can't fulfill the call?

We are saying "we're going up-up-up" - but what are you willing to commit wholeheartedly to? What is it going to take to help you ascend upward? Sometimes, God must do us like the eagle does to its young – give it a push, so it can fly. If we are not willing to take that leap of faith on our own to fulfill God's call on our lives, "guess what?" – God is not going to be lacking anything. If we don't ascend to a higher level, it will be us on the losing end. God can use someone else to get the job done or something else. Remember what God said in his word in Luke 19:40-44 If you don't praise me, a rock will take your place. God will never be left without a witness, it's best that we obey, do more than just be a bench warmer, lingering in stagnation, there is much to be done in the kingdom of God, we have a responsibility to get the job done. Why did God give us His Holy Spirit (power), if we're not going to use it?

ASCENSION ATTENTION #2:
SPIRITUAL PUSH

The apostles couldn't stay just in Jerusalem to minister the gospel, they had to expand, grow, go to a higher level. God had to give them a nudge, so the gospel could spread to all the world- Acts 15:37-41 (ESV). We, as God's agents or disciples must respond to the call of God to go higher, grow, to ascend. Whatever you are anointed to do to cause heaven to come to earth, ask God to increase your faith for your territory of witness. We must ascend to a higher level if we want the words of the Lord's prayer to manifest. Matthew 6:10 (ESV) says, for God's will to be done on earth, as it is in heaven, it's our job to make it happen. Heaven is not coming to earth until we ascend to a higher level of kingdom work in the earth. We must move upward. We must grow. We must go higher. We will ascend to a higher level, in the name of the Lord Jesus. Amen.

NADINE GAMBLE

ASCENSION ATTENTION #3–
RISE TO A HIGHER LEVEL

Elevate your mind. Think of yourself the way Christ thought of himself. Let this mind be in you, which was also in Christ Jesus, Philippians 2:5-11 MSG

We will soar, climb, and proceed upward to a superior level. We will elevate our minds.

We will live and operate in the presence of God through His revelation by the Holy Spirit. We have a strong belief for change that will align our hearts and minds with the will of God.

We will ascend to that which is sacred, holy, and dedicated to God's higher purpose.

We will keep our eyes on Jesus.

We will receive revelation from God through prayer, meditation, and reading His Word.

We will pursue wisdom.

We will receive God's favor. God is calling us to a higher level in Him.

I have extraordinary distinction that sets me apart for God.

I will stay focused and submit to God's will.

I will pursue God's idea for my life. Oh, Lord, help us to stay in constant pursuit of your righteousness to advance your Kingdom.

We are submitted and committed to being your disciples, your agents, and your ambassadors in the earth.

It is so in the name of Jesus Christ, Amen.

LIVING IN GOD'S LOVE

Help us all, Lord, in everything we do, to represent you as your sons and daughters. Father God, help us to contribute, to walk, surrender to the extravagant love of Christ. His great love was pleasing to you Father God, like an aroma of adoration, a sweet healing fragrance. Oh Lord, we are your holy ones. We keep ourselves from worthless words that bring disgrace and dishonor to your name. Bless us, O Lord, with worship words to fill our hearts. Spill out and manifest your love. Oh Lord, I confess I would not be guilty of the impure things that defile your Kingdom. I confess I will live a life of abundant righteousness through you Lord Jesus Christ.

I declare I am one big bundle of submitted, committed, obedient consuming fire to all unrighteousness. Father God, I'm thankful I'm living in your love. Your love conquers all. Oh Lord, I confess my deeds and character mimic yours. I am filled with your thoughts and your love.

Lord, help us to live our lives your way so the perfect example of the love you require can be seen in us because the most effective sermon we will ever preach is our lives. In Jesus name, Amen.

LIVING IN GOD'S WISDOM

See, then, that you walk circumspectly, not as fools but as wise, redeeming the times because the days are evil. Ephesians 5:15-16 KJV

Oh Lord helps us to be careful how we live.

Father God, help us to value time and not waste it on useless work.

Bless us, Lord Jesus, with your wisdom to live successfully in these end times.

Help us oh Lord, to live our lives, to fulfill Your divine purpose and will.

Thank you, Lord, for giving us your discernment to fully understand Your will.

Bless us, Lord Jesus, through Your Holy Spirit, to open our hearts to you, so we can possess the stability and soberness needed to make wise decisions.

Lord Jesus, thank you for giving us a desire to seek, to be full of your Holy Spirit, so our hearts will overflow with joy and gladness. Now, Holy Spirit fill us so the name of Jesus will be praised and glorified.

Lord Jesus, help us to take advantage of every chance we get to reverence You and support each other in love.

Lord Jesus, thank you for giving us Your wisdom to know that loving and obeying you is the essence of an abundant, joy filled life.

Thank you, Jesus. Amen.

IN HIS PRESENCE

You make known to me the path of life in your presence. There is fullness of joy at your right hand and pleasures forevermore. Psalm 16:11 ESV

Oh Lord, I stand in awe of your beauty and your splendor.

Lord Jesus, my soul longs to live in your presence where I can experience the fullness of your joy and blessings.

Lord, your loving words are like the honeycomb to me. I find the promised land flowing from within you.

Oh Lord, you are so wonderful.

Thank you, Lord Jesus, for the times of refreshing which enters in from your presence.

Lord Jesus, your presence will go with me and give me rest.

Oh, Lord. I look for you with all my heart, and I find you.

Lord Jesus, you are near to me and not far away.

Lord Jesus, make my heart pure so I can see you.

Jesus, I can't live without you. Thank you for your promise to never leave me.

Father God, you are the God of my salvation. I will wait for you all day long.

Oh Lord, you are in our midst. We rejoice with joy and gladness.

Lord Jesus, it is good to be near you, you will quiet us with your love.

Oh, Lord, I delight myself in you. You are my desire.

Thank you, Jesus, it's in you that I live and abide under your shadow.

Oh Lord, I'm asking you this one thing, to live with you in your house forever, so I can look upon your beauty.

I love you, Jesus. Amen.

FEARLESS FAITH

The Lord is my helper; I will not fear; what can man to do me? Hebrews 13:6 ESV

The Lord is my light and my salvation; whom shall, I fear? Psalm 27:1 ESV

Oh Lord, you are my light to guide me along the way. I fear no one.

Lord Jesus, you are the source of my salvation to defend me every day.

Thank you, Lord, for being my protection when evil comes to destroy me, my heart will not be afraid.

Even if an army rises to attack me., Lord Jesus, you are with me.

Lord Jesus, I know you are there to help me, so I will not be shaken.

Oh, Lord, I will not allow fear to paralyze my ability to live by faith.

Lord Jesus, in your shelter in the day of trouble is where I will be found.

For you lord God Almighty, Will hide me in your protective arms.

Father God, you have always hidden me in your secret place where I am kept safe and secure from all my enemies.

Oh Lord, now I bring you my offering of praise in the name of Jesus Christ. Amen.

MY STRENGTH AND MY SHIELD

Blessed be the Lord! For he has heard the voice of my pleas for mercy. The Lord is my strength and my shield, in him my heart trusts, and I am helped. Psalms 28:6-7 ESV

Lord Jesus, I am coming to you asking for help, letting you know what I need.

Oh, Lord, can't you see my turning toward your mercy seat?

To you Oh Lord, I lift my hands and surrender to prayer.

Oh, Lord, listen to my cries. You have answered my prayers for mercy before. Lord Jesus, do it again.

Lord Jesus, you are my strength and shield from danger.
Help me to fully trust you Lord Jesus, so I will know help is on the way.

Thank you, Jesus, for being the inner strength of all your people.

Lord Jesus, you are a mighty protection over everyone.

Lord Jesus, you are the saving strength for all your anointed ones.

Lord Jesus in you we will never fail.

Lord Jesus, like a shepherd going before us, keep leading us forward forever, carrying us in your arms.

Thank you, Jesus.

Amen.

THE MAJESTY OF GOD

On the glorious splendor of your majesty, and on your wondrous works, I will meditate. They shall speak of the might of your awesome deeds, and I will declare your greatness. Psalm 145:5-6 ESV

Oh Lord, you reign as King, you have covered yourself with majesty and strength.

Lord God Almighty, you have reigned as King from the very beginning of time; Eternity is your home.

O Lord, at the sound of your voice, everything chaotic is calmed and becomes peaceful.

Lord Jesus, you are our majestic King filled with awesome power, nothing can change your rules, they will last forever.

Holiness is the beauty that fills your house.

Lord Jesus, you are royalty and greatness in all your splendor and glory.

Father, Lord, Your glorious majesty streams from the heavens.

Lord God Almighty, your divine order joins the earth to the heavens to bring the heavenly glory into the earth, making the heaven and earth one. Father God Almighty, People everywhere see your majesty, what glory streams from the heavens, filling the earth with the fame of your name.

Hallelujah. Amen!

GOD'S CONSTANT LOVE

Many waters cannot quench love, neither can floods drown it. Song of Solomon 8:7 ESV

He brought me to the Banquet House, and his banner over me was love. Song of Solomon 2:4 ESV

That everyone gives all praise and thanks to the Lord, because His love never runs out.

Let's praise our God, because He is better than anyone could ever imagine.

Our God is always loving, kind and faithful. His love is so rich, pure, marvelous and strong.

Go ahead, let everyone know it, how he delivered us from the power of darkness, when we were desperate and filled with hopelessness and despair, we cried, "Oh, Lord help us, rescue us!" and he did. Thank you, Lord, for delivering us when we were prisoners of our pain.

Thank you, Lord, for being a doctor in our sickness and afflictions.

Lord God Almighty, you spoke the words, "be healed" and it happened.

Oh, Lord, thank you. For all your miracles and mercy for those you love. Lift your hands and give thanks to God, our Father, Savior and friend. For his wonderful kindness for those whom he loves.

Let us exalt him on high; lift up your praise unto the Lord.

Let all the people know how great our God is. There is no greater love.

Hallelujah. Thank you, Jesus. Amen.

I AM A SON

For all who are led by the Spirit of God, are sons of God. For you did not receive the spirit of slavery to fall back into fear, but you have received the spirit of adoption as sons, by whom we cry, "Abba! Father!" Romans 8:14-15 ESV

As a son, I have a special relationship with God.

As a son, all obstacles that stand in my way, my God will handle.

I am a Son of God, in pursuit of a Kingdom mindset.

I am a son of God; I seek God's original thoughts and purpose for my life.

I am a son of God. I am built and have a purpose. I am a Son of God; I am an idea for his glory.

I am a son of God. I have my identity restored through Jesus Christ. (Galatians 4:4-5 ESV)

I am a son of God; I have full rights to be restored to what I was before sin.

I am a son of God, delivered from ignorance of who my enemy is. I am the Son of God, rescued and delivered from distraction. As a son of God, Jesus is my supreme deliverer. I know the difference between freedom and deliverance. Thank you, Lord Jesus, I am a son and have been made aware of that deliverance. He Prepares me for freedom, which delivers me from oppression.

Glory to your name, oh Lord. Amen.

CHAPTER 2

· + + ◆ + + ·

OBJECT OF
GOD'S LOVE

The greatest robbery of all time is when the enemy blinds you to your true identity. Your identity as a child of God comes with gifts, purpose, and inheritance. In fact, those who exercise their faith through prayer and the power of the Word of God can recognize their true identity; therefore, they are destined to fulfill God's purpose with Victory! It is this scenario that the enemy fears. God declares in his word that we are more than conquerors and we are victorious to overcome the world no matter what circumstance we find ourselves in. 1 John 5:4 (KJV) states, "for whatsoever is born of God over-cometh the world: and this is the victory that overcometh the world, even our faith". Rest assured, God has never suffered a defeat, nor will he ever! He has given each of us the power to overcome ANYTHING the enemy throws at us. Luke 10:19 (KJV) states, "behold, I give you power to tread on serpents and scorpions, and over all the power of the enemy; and nothing shall by any means hurt you". The enemy is banking on keeping you blinded. Do you know your purpose? If not, it is time to have a conversation with the one who created you and predestined your purpose from the moment you were born.

I AM

Since God the Father calls His Son the Beloved, which is evidence of his love for Him, and since believers are in Christ, we are also the object of God's love.

To the days of His glorious grace, with which he has blessed us in the Beloved. Ephesians 1:6 **Scriptures ESV**

I AM...	
Loved	Ephesians 3:16-19
Redeemed	1Peter 1:18; Galatians 3:13
Kingdom	Exodus 19:5-6; Revelation 1:5-6
Justified	Romans 5:1-19
Honored	Psalms 19:16
Chosen	Ephesians 1:4; 1Peter 2:9
Called	Philippians 3:14
Treasured	Deuteronomy 26:18-19
Healed	I Peter 2:24
Delivered	Colossians 1:13
Light	Matthew 5:14-16
Holy	Ephesians 1:4
Royalty	I Peter 2:9; Exodus 19:5-6
Free	Romans 8:1-2; John 8:36
Protected	Psalms 37:7; Psalms 4:8; Psalms 91
Covered	Ephesians 2:13
Hidden	Colossians 3:3
Safe	Proverbs 18:10
Blessed	Ephesians 1:6
Sealed	Ephesians 1:3

Accepted	Ephesians 1:6
Complete	Colossians 2:10
Satisfied	Psalms 63:3-5
Comforted	Philippians 4:6-7
Known	Matthew 10:30
Rescued	II Samuel 22:17-20
Adopted	Romans 8:15-17

GOD SAID

Timely advice is lovely, like golden apples in a silver basket. Proverbs 25:11 NLT

Heavenly Father, help us to speak your words of wisdom.

Help us to believe that if we say it according to your word, we will see it.

Oh Lord, your word says death and life are in the power of the tongue.

Lord Jesus, help us to use wise words when we speak.

Bless us Lord Jesus, to say in faith what you have said.

When we speak, our words will not be self-sabotaging, aborting our blessings. Lord Jesus, help us to speak words that are life giving and not life taking.

We declare and decree we will not say words that take our own lives or the lives of others. We will speak words that add life with your help.

Help us, Lord Jesus, to take responsibility for the words we say.

Help us, Lord, to change the negatives into positives in what we say.

Holy Spirit, give us revelation knowledge to say the right words.

In the name of the Lord Jesus, Amen.

HEART FIXER

Create in me a clean heart Oh God. Renew a loyal spirit in me. Psalms 51:10 NLT. Allow the Holy Spirit to work in us to provide soundness and soberness to navigate through life. Psalms 51:10-12 ESV

Lord Jesus, fix my heart, so my praises ring out in joyful adoration to glorify your name.

Lord Jesus, fix my mind, so I will be intentional in my praise.

Fix my heart Lord, so Your grace and mercy will show up and show out in my life

Fix my heart, Lord, So I will seek your Kingdom first.

Fix my heart, Lord, so the light of your love can be seen by those in bondage and captivity, that they may experience your chain breaking love of deliverance.

Fix my heart Lord, so all nations will experience the glorious presence of your love and compassion

Fix my heart Lord, so your plan for my life will not be hijacked or derailed.

Fix my heart, Lord, so the mind of Christ will be seen in me.

Fix my heart Lord, so I will worship you without restraint.

Thank you, Jesus. Amen.

THIRSTING FOR GOD

With passion, I pursue and cling to you because I feel your pleasant grip on my life. I will keep my soul close to your heart. Psalm 63:8 TPT

Oh Lord God of my life in this weary wilderness I'm in, I thirst for you. Lord Jesus, there is such a craving in my heart for you. I can't describe, I thirst for you.

Lord Jesus, there is such a yearning that grips my soul for you. I thirst for you

Oh Lord, I am energized every time I enter your heavenly sanctuary to seek more of you, I thirst for you.

Lord Jesus, your tender mercies mean more to me than life itself. I thirst for you.

How I love and praise you, my God. I thirst for you, Lord

Daily, I will worship you with all my heart. I thirst for you, Oh Lord God.

I overflow with praise when I come before you.

Lord Jesus, I thirst for you.

Oh Lord, the anointing of your presence satisfies me like nothing else. I thirst for you. Lord Jesus, I keep my soul close to your heart. I thirst for you.

Glory Hallelujah. Amen.

CONFORM NOT TO THE WORLD

And when I am lifted up from the earth, I will draw everyone unto myself. John 12:32 NLT

Lord Jesus, help us to never convert the Church to the world; but to you alone. We confess, Lord Jesus, we will live in such a way that men will be drawn to you. Lord Jesus, we lift up truth.

We will not lose because we teach the truth. We are fighting from victory. You have won the battle on the cross...It is Finish!

Lord Jesus, help our church members, the saints of the most high God to be stable and do not drift.

When we teach the truth of your Word, Lord Jesus, we declare we have stability because we are rooted and grounded in the Word of God.

Lord Jesus, your word attracts old and young to God. The Word of God is truth, and the truth sets free.

Lord Jesus, help us to realize, just doing, church in a building does not reach the masses of drawing all people to Christ.

Lord Jesus, help us to follow your order and lift you up so a lost and dying world can receive your eternal salvation, in the name of the Lord Jesus Christ, Amen.

THE GREATEST GIFT

Now, thanks be to God. For his indescribable gift [which is precious beyond words]! 2 Corinthians 9:15 AMP

Father God, thank you for showing love and compassion to us.

Lord God Almighty, you sent to Earth, your greatest gift.

Oh Lord, we are grateful that you gave us the gift of yourself wrapped in flesh, Jesus Christ the Son.

Father God, thank you for the miracle birth! None like it nor ever will be.

Oh Lord God, you are an awesome God, fulfilling your promises of old. Your promises are always sure. The virgin bore a son!

Father God, you gave him a name, Emmanuel, meaning our God is with us.

Father God, thank you, there is none - and never will be a gift so great as this one.

Thank you, Father God, this gift will never lose its value.

Thank you, Father God, this gift can and will keep on giving.

Holy Father, we will forever praise your great name! For this significant gift, it's too wonderful for words!

Thank you, Heavenly Father, for giving us your perfect gift.

Lord God our father, Amen.

GOD'S PERFECT ANGER

Oh Lord, don't rebuke me in your anger or discipline me in your rage. Have compassion on me, Lord for I am weak. Heal me Lord, for my bones are in agony. Psalms 6:1-2 NLT

Lord God Almighty, you are perfect in all your ways, even when you are angry, it's still working for our good.

Father God, thank you; your anger is a righteous anger.

Father Lord, your anger is not a destructive but a corrective power to those who love and serve you.

Thank you, Lord God, for correcting me with your perfect anger. We learn, oh Lord, your perfect anger delivers my life from evil.

Lord God, help us to be like you and channel our anger into a burning passion to spread the gospel.

Thank you, Father God, that when your anger is stirred, it becomes your plan to have fellowship with the human race, not in conflict with us.

The Lord is slow to anger and great in power. And he will by no means leave the guilty unpunished. (Nahum 1:3 AMP)

Our God is powerful, but it's a patient power.

Thank you, Jesus. Amen.

DYING TO LIVE

I have been crucified with Christ. It is no longer I who live, but Christ who lives in me and the life I now live in the flesh. I live by faith in the Son of God who loved me and gave himself for me. Galatians 2:20 ESV

The disciple Paul knew that to live is Christ and to die to our sin is gain. Count it all gain that we may win Christ. Phil 1:21 KJV. You living a Godly life as God purposed brings glory to God and your life of sacrifice brings an assurance of faith that what we lose in this life is small compared to the gain in heaven.

An invitation to die is an invitation to live. Father God, help your people to know that dying to ourselves is essential in your Kingdom.

Lord Jesus, thank you, I have been crucified with you and I am no longer a slave to sin, but have been set free. Oh Lord, thank you, that the life I now live in the body, I live by faith in you.

Thank you, Jesus, you love me and gave your life for me.

Thank you, Lord, I'm being shaped into your likeness

Lord Jesus, I want to become a carbon copy and a masterpiece of your making

Pour me out Lord Jesus, help me to become a diamond so your reflection can be seen in me.

Oh Lord, help me to be like a caterpillar who gave up its old way of life to become a work of magnificent beauty.

Lord Jesus, help me to surrender my plans, desires and gifts to you for your purpose for my life. Oh Lord, realign my plans, reshape my desires, repurpose my gifts for your glory.

Lord Jesus, help us to come to you as we are, and we give you permission to transform and renew our lives.

In the name of Jesus Christ, Amen.

JESUS OUR ONLY HOPE

"Rejoice in hope, be patient in tribulation, be constant in prayer." Romans 12:2 ESV

Lord Jesus, you are our only hope.

Lord Jesus, open our eyes. Focus us on your Kingdom hope.

Oh Lord, remove any blindness that hinders our focus of you

Change our nature, oh Lord, where our lives are full of hope. We don't throw away our confidence in you, Lord Jesus. You are our rich reward.

We say yes to you, Lord, you are our steadfast hope.

We declare and decree, we will not fail, O Lord, we hope in you.

Because of your resurrection, Lord Jesus, we have a living hope.

Lord Jesus, because of you we are prepared to live and not die a spiritual death.

We confess Lord Jesus dead hope is not our conclusion; death is not the end.

Lord Jesus, I lift my eyes to you, all I have or ever hope to be. I owe all to you. I declare I will not faint under pressure because I hope in the Lord.

I confess all my weary days are over, I hope in the Lord.

In you, Lord Jesus. I have a hope for a future that can't be lost or spoiled.

All praise to our Lord and Savior Jesus Christ, I put my trust in you.

Lord Jesus, you are my eternal hope who gives me the victory.

Hallelujah. Thank you, Jesus. Amen.

DON'T WORRY

Trust in the Lord with all your heart and do not lean on your own understanding. In all your ways acknowledge Him and He will make straight your paths. Proverbs 3:5-6 ESV

Worrying does not change things but places a focus on the problem and allows our enemy access to personify the situation for his gain. For example, anxiety or depression can manifest into physical sickness or expressing fear that makes you act outside of your character. Take everything, and I mean everything, small and great to God. What God can do in a second is beyond a miracle. We have no idea how much God gets done in a moment for us each day. With God the impossible becomes possible. Take it to God, from small decisions to great...what to cook today to healing of a loved one. It all matters to Him. His hands

are much greater to handle the problems of yesterday, today, and tomorrow. Remember He is the Almighty Eternal Everlasting God who has already seen your yesterday, today, and tomorrow. Time was created for man, but God lives in eternity, so He is not bound by time. Since He is Omnipresent, Omniscience, Omnipotent, He sees everything all in once glance. Trust me when I say, God is already working on your situation; it will turn in your favor because He is the same God yesterday, today, and forever. Heb 13:8 ESV

Lord Jesus, I declare, I will not worry, because the Kingdom is in you. I am a citizen in your kingdom.

Lord Jesus what you think about me is a reality in my life.

Father God, whatever you think about me is who I am.

I declare I have spiritual wholeness in your Kingdom, Lord.

I declare and decree I am prosperous and in a healthy place, body, mind and spirit.

Kingdom prosperity is a prepared place. Jesus provides for me, and I lack nothing.

Thank you, King Jesus, you are committed to see that I have all your Kingdom provisions.

Oh Lord, I trust your government overall.

Thank you, Jesus, you oversee sustaining Kingdom prosperity.

Oh Lord, I will not worry. I put my trust in you.

Lord Jesus, I confess I will not yield when the enemy shows up and attacks my trust.

I declare my trust level in you, O Lord, is the lens I see through.

Lord Jesus, I speak. You are going to take care of me when the drought and famine come.

I don't worry about poverty. I have everything I need in the King's Kingdom. It's mine.

I am your responsibility, Lord Jesus. I trust the King for my well-being. He is a responsible for taking care of me.

I will stop settling for defeat, because all God's stories end in victory

I confess the job of worry outranks me. That job is for God, not me. He will come, He promised to help me.

Thank you, Jesus. Amen.

HONOR THE KING, DO IT NOW!

You will always have the poor among you, but you will not always have me. John 12:8 NLV

Lord Jesus, make us tender to your presence.

Father, Lord, help us to be anxious to catch a glimpse of Jesus.

Help us, Lord, to pack our minds and hearts with things we forgot about who you are.

Fling the doors wide so Jesus can be on display and call people to Himself. Through our lives we live each day.

Oh Lord, help us to lift you up until you speak from eternity, so that every ear will hear, and every eye will see; until all fall prostate before you, worshipping you on bended knee.

Our lights, oh Lord, help us to let shine, to dispel every darkness until we triumph in victory, and all is truly thine.

All to you Jesus, I surrender; humbly at your feet I bow

Worldly pleasures all forsaken.

Take me Jesus, take me now

In Jesus Christ's name, Amen.

HOW BIG IS GOD?

I am the Alpha and the Omega, says the Lord God, who is and who was and who is to come, the Almighty. Revelation 1:8 ESV

Oh Lord, you are bigger than the killer blow that was dealt to us in Eden.

When the second Adam came, and our enemy was beaten.

Bigger than the deepest sea? Who's billows roll

Bigger than what men value in silver and gold.

Bigger than the mountains that stand strong in our life

Bigger than the battle that are raging through strife.

Bigger than Satan's arrows that fly by night

Bigger than any weapon formed to kill, steal and destroy my life.

Bigger than any wilderness I am going through

Bigger than any giant that's threatening too

How great are you, Almighty God, Savior, Lord and friend

You're delivering power, O Lord, on it we can depend

Your love Lord Jesus is so deep, so wide, so marvelous and strong

It will forever more endure. The Saints and angels' sing.

Father, Lord, you are bigger than this mighty universe, but small enough to live within my heart.

Amen. Amen. Amen.

STRONG FAITH

For we walk by faith, not by sight. 2Corinthians 5:7 KJV

Lord Jesus, I declare I'm walking by faith, not by sight.

I confess faith is my lifestyle behavior that the enemy is targeting in my life.

I declare I Will Survive any beating I receive in my threshing.

I declare the enemy who is not after my stuff but after my faith will not win it.

I nullify anything in my life that's working against my faith

I declare faith is my life and whatever I do is infused by.

I confess, the oxygen of faith is why I really am living.

I acknowledge that everything in your Kingdom, O Lord, is received by faith, I received nothing without it.

I declare whatever I do is to be infused by faith, because faith is the currency of your kingdom.

Oh Lord, remove any doubt, fear and sin from me.

I will not walk like the living dead. The dead is not where I go for my future.

Lord Jesus, get involved so I can have strong faith.

Oh Lord, your word says fight the good fight of faith. The battle is fought for my faith, oh Lord, and it's in you I put my trust to win this one for me.

Thank you, Jesus. Amen.

THE GLORY RETURN

...As soon as you see the Ark of the Covenant of the Lord, your God being carried by the Levitical priests, then you shall set out from your place and follow it. Joshua.3:3 ESV

Thank you, Lord God, your glory is coming back.

Teach us, oh Lord, how to handle your glory.

Father God, your glory always changes the atmosphere of things and situations.

Thank you, Oh Lord God, we bear your glory because you are present in US.

Father, Lord, shape our lives to show your glory is inside us.

Work in us, oh Lord, so your glory will show up in your people.

Help us, oh Lord, to feast in your glory.

Oh Lord, your glory is what I desire to live in me. Your presence is where your glory hangs out.

I am hungry, O Lord, for your illuminating light, so splendorous and bright.

Lord Jesus, let me always live in the presence of where you are.

Bathing me in the glorious perfume of your holy fire.

Oh Lord, I can't live without you. Occupy the totality of who I am.

A little dab won't do me. I want as much of you as I can have.

Thank you, Jesus.

KNOWN BY OUR SCARS

He was pierced for our transgressions. He was crushed for our iniquities. Upon him was the chastisement that brought us peace. And with his wounds we are healed. Isaiah 53:5 ESV

Lord Jesus, we have been crucified with you. We bear your DNA.

The scars you carry on your body have opened the way.

We are known by the scars through life's tragedies, disappointments and pain.

On this laborious journey, eternal life to gain.

Known by the scars of living a sacrificial life.

Marred by the scars of misery and strife.

I carry the cross of my savior who suffered many scars.

He endured until the end so we would win the wars.

My life is a never-ending fight that will produce many scars.

But like our Lord and Savior, the church is recognized by its scars.

Praise your holy name, Lord Jesus, Amen.

SITTING AT JESUS' FEET

Oh Lord, I love the habitation of your house and the place where your glory dwells. Psalms 26:8 ESV

Sitting at Jesus feet gives me joy like nothing else can.

Sitting at Jesus feet moves me into a trouble Freeland.

Sitting at Jesus feet, I'm embraced in his love and kindness; so tender and sweet.

In his awesome presence I experienced peace complete.

Sitting at Jesus feet I look full into his wonderful face.

And the cares of this life grow dim because of his glory and grace.

Sitting at Jesus feet, I confess I have everything I need

Jesus is the abundant source on which I feed.

Tomorrow is not a worry because I know who holds my hand

When I sit at Jesus feet, he studies me to stand.

Lord Jesus, I love sitting at your feet

And the beauty of your holiness each day when we meet.

At your feet, dear Jesus, is where you reveal your perfect plan

Where you bring all together concerning God and man.

Hallelujah, Amen.

SWEET HOUR OF PRAYER

(Song)

Sweet hour of prayer. Sweet hour of prayer

That calls me from a world of care

It bids me at my Father's throne

Make all my wants and wishes known

And seasons of distress and grief

My soul has often found relief

And off escape the tempter snare

By that return, sweet hour of prayer

Sweet hour of prayer, sweet hour of prayer

The joys I feel, the bliss I share, of those whose anxious spirits burn

With strong desire for thy return

With such, I hasten to the place

Where Jesus my Savior shows his face

And gladly take my station there

And wait for thee, sweet hour of prayer

Sweet hour of prayer. Sweet hour of prayer.

Thy wings shall my petition bear to him whose truth and faithfulness

Engage the waiting soul to bless

And since he bids me seek his face.

Believe His word and trust His grace

I'll cast on him my every care

And wait for the sweet hour of prayer.

Author W.W. Walford (1845)

PRAY

And He spake a parable unto them to this end, that men ought always to pray, and not to faint. Luke. 18:1 KJV

When it all seems to be falling apart, and I can't find my way. When the struggle seemed too much to bear, I pray

During those times when trials and tribulations on me weigh. When I don't know what to do anymore, I pray.

If I feel that my strength has fled, that my joy has turned to dismay and I don't have anywhere to turn, I pray

When I stand tall on my knees, I fall.

When I need to be lifted high, I bow down low in front of my Lord

Prostate I lay

When all hope is gone, I pray.

My Lord hears me

Crying out to Him every day

He patiently waits on me to call Him

Patiently waits on me to pray

He dries my tears and eases my fears. From His love I can never stray.

All it takes is a heartfelt word

All I have to do is pray

I go to God on bended knees.

Without hesitation or delay

I go to my loving Father

He will listen if I pray.

Author Timothy Jones.

CHAPTER 3

AN ASCENDED LIFE

LIVING AN ASCENDED LIFE

So, Jesus said, "I speak to you eternal truth. The Son is unable to do anything of himself or through his own initiative. I only do the works that I see the father doing, for the son does the same works as his Father." John 5:19 TPT

What kind of life do you desire to have? Proverbs 18:21 KJV says, "death and life are in the power of the tongue: and they that love it shall eat the fruit thereof". Living an ascended life has been given to us freely and we have His power to do so. It truly is a mindset to having the faith to step out to live as the Word of God says. Is it easy? The word says otherwise. He didn't promise the road would be easy, but He did promise that He would be with us always and never leave us. We have The Helper through God. My daughter works in healthcare and often says, the rhythm of your heart on a monitor show that you are alive. The ups and downs of the beating heart is life. Place your hand on your heart. Can you feel the beat of life...beep beep...beep beep? A flat line means death! Just like that heartbeat, life will be up one minute then down the next. It shows that you are alive and living through your peaks and valleys. Rest assured that when you are down you will rise again, just like that heartbeat. If we never had hard times, how would you build a trust in God or know He exist? If you never experienced loneliness or hurt, how would you know the beauty of companionship and peace? Now, look back over your life and look to see all the times where God was there to get you through or at times even carried you. What love! Psalms 23 makes a promise that God will be with you; "Yeah, though I walk through the valley of the shadow of death, I will fear no evil; for thou art with me; thy rod and thy staff they comfort me. (psalm 23: 4 KJV). God is with you in the valley as well. Get your mind to wrap around that for a moment. The light of God is with you even when mountains try to overshadow and take away the light. Even grass grows in a valley and rest assured, God will rescue you and make it right. Ascending your thoughts to know that God will take care of you, brings about growth to lead you to living an ascended life.

There is a life prepared for us by Father God the Creator. It's not just to make us happy, but for us to live an ascended life. A life filled with the power and promises of Jesus Christ.

Jesus lived an ascended life. A bodily return to heaven (John 5:19) KJV paraphrased

I Decree and declare I have the mind of Christ. Everything in my life will take me to a higher level.

My confession is I will rise to a higher level. I will go upward.

I will live my lifestyle from a higher level.

How I function will look like heaven.

I have proper activities and actions that's not focused on what's happening here, but things of heaven.

I depend on God, my Heavenly Father, for focus.

My Heavenly Father already knows all my needs.

I confess I am already taken care of because I seek the Kingdom of God and His righteousness.

I am not going to worry because it's not my job.

I don't need to be in control because God already is.

I will seek him, I will submit, I will ascend.

Oh Lord, help me to submit my eyes so I can see like you

I will submit my eyes to you, O Lord, so I won't be spiritually blind.

I confess I am safe because I submit to God's level of submission.

I am satisfied because I am submitted and committed.

Thank you, Jesus, for adding your blessings of favor because I am submitted to you with all that I am.

I will experience the blessings of an ascended life because I am obedient.

Thank you, Jesus. Amen.

POWER FOR THE ZERO HOUR

But ye shall receive power after that the Holy Ghost is come upon you. Acts 1:8 KJV

Thank you, Heavenly Father, for your awesome power. It's there to sustain me in my zero hour.

Prayer, praise, and worship are my constant friends.

They are closer than a brother.

On them I can depend.

When all things around me presents like sinking sand

Praise, prayer, and worship are there to lend a helping hand.

No matter the time or season or what may come my way

Prayer, praise, and worship are there without delay.

When enemies are threatening like a consuming flood

I call prayer, praise, and worship my voice by them are heard.

Prayer, praise, and worship, on them I can depend

They are near as a whisper

Always ready to defend.

Prayer, praise, and worship. There's no greater power

That can give to us the victory in our zero hour.

Glory. Amen

A PRAYER OF PROTECTION

Those who live in the shelter of the Most High will find rest in the shadow of the Almighty. This I declare about the Lord: He alone is my refuge, my place of safety; He is my God, and I trust Him. Psalms 91:1-2 NLT

Oh Lord God, who hears my prayers, listen to my heart's cry

No matter where I am.

I will cry out to you for a father's help.

My strength is found when I wait upon you.

Watch over me, Father God, you are my fortress.

When I am feeble and overwhelmed, guide me into your glory where I am safe and sheltered

Lord, you are a paradise of protection to me.

You lift me high where my enemies cannot touch me.

Oh Lord, let me live forever in your sanctuary safely

Beneath the shelter of your wings

Keep me in your glory

Guard me Father God, with your unending, unfailing love.

Let me live day by day, walking in grace and truth before you.

You, O Lord, are my safe place

Your presence always protects me. Lord Jesus, you are my defender.

I will not let worry paralyze me.

Your glory, O Lord, is all around me.

There is no risk of failure with you, my God

For you Lord, are my Savior, my hero, and my life-giving strength.

It's in you, O Lord, I put my trust.

In Jesus Christ's name, Amen

CHAPTER 4

THE POWER OF PRAYER

THE PURPOSE OF PRAYER

Trust in the Lord with all your heart; do not depend on your own understanding. Seek his will and in all you do, and he will show you which path to take. Proverbs 3:5-6 NLT

First, what is purpose? Purpose is something set up as an object or end to be attained; intention, resolution, determination, something you mean to do or accomplish; a goal; something you're trying to reach for.

Today that goal for us should be a desire to be like Jesus.

God has given us the tools to fulfill the purpose He has for each of us; however, our experiences in life often drive us away from this purpose and molds us into what we are today. Often confused and misguided to the point we no longer know what our purpose is. Many of us will spend a lifetime searching for our purpose and feel it is so elusive that it is unattainable. The goal of the World is to first mold, then label, and finally

categorize you in a way that limits your true potential. Never allow the world to define who you are knowing that The Word of God is the blueprint that reveals all that you are capable of accomplishing. God has created us in his image; therefore, his favor is in our DNA. God has provided an inheritance that offers a life of protection, advocacy, provisions, and the gift of everlasting life. 1Corithians 10:26-27 (KJV) says, the earth is the Lord's and the fullness thereof. Only God knows our path and only he can provide the directions to our final destination; we merely have to choose to walk the path he's laid out for each of us! "Therefore, you are no longer a slave, but a son; and if a son, then an heir through God". Galatians 4:7 (NKJV). We are the children of God and the object of His affection. Believe that!

<u>Prayer</u> is talking to God and him talking back to you. It is a two-way conversation between the Father and His child.

God is the one who gives us purpose and only through God is our purpose obtainable.

We need to have a connection with God.

We should aim to fulfill our purpose through Christ Jesus as He gives us direction.

For that to happen, we must have a relationship with God. That means we must pray to talk to God.

As people of God, we need to value that relationship highly.

It's the key to success for the people of God.

Have you ever thought what would happen if we didn't talk to God?

We will never fulfill our purpose. If we don't talk to God, everything will fall apart.

God said without me you can do nothing. (John 15:5)

God says in all our ways, consult Him so he can reveal to us what to do. (Proverbs. 3:5-6).

We might as well admit it, we are a mess without God's direction.

That's why we need to value our relationship with God.

We as people of God have a tendency to be drifters; neither hot nor cold. Sometimes we slide back or become self-serving.

Me, myself, and I is our focus instead of Jesus being the object of our affection.

Not seeking the good in others, short sighted, judgmental, immature, not serious about our relationship with God.

PURPOSE OF PRAYER #2

God wants to change us into his kind of people that's filled with justice, mercy and faith. People who have Christ's mind. (Galatians 5:22-23)

Prayer is a way to align our minds with Christ's mind.

Prayer is also a conscious attempt to experience the presence of God, to be with him. Prayer heightens our connection with God's mind. (Philippians 2:4-5)

To bring forth:

1. Holiness (being like God)
2. Wisdom – knowledge, good judgment
3. Healing - Well-being, not just physical.
4. Prosperity. – success, thriving, flourishing

People of God, we have a responsibility to seek God for change that is needed to make us like Him.

We must pray. 2Chronicles 7:14 teaches us how to get the job of prayer done. Jeremiah 29:12 Gives us information on praying: We must pray.

The scriptures say:

1. Pray always (1 Thessalonians 5:16-17)
2. Pray much (James 5:6)
3. Pray about everything (Philippians 4:6)

I've heard this word spoken of about prayer: Prayer is a vital breath. It is our lifeline.

That means prayer is necessary for us to live spiritually.

It is vital to the process of fulfilled purpose.

Prayer changes us, our awareness, our thoughts, our perception, our thinking, and as a result our behavior changes and then our lives.

We become better after we pray because now, we see with God's understanding.

WHAT PRAYER DOES NOT ACCOMPLISH

Prayer does not change God; just in case you thought it did.

Our prayers do not change other people.

Other people may seem to change; however, through prayer our perception and understanding of them change. They may change in response of our new perception and understanding of them, after we have been with Jesus and prayed.

The change we may see will result from the change in their perception of us.

They will love when we change.

What is our most famous prayer? Lord, change the other person! When in fact, it's probably us who needs to change.

Sometimes we focus on other people's faults instead of our own, when in fact is, "it's me, Oh Lord that needs to change.

HOW TO PRAY FOR MYSELF?

When I am weak, the Holy Spirit takes over in me to intercede on my behalf, pleading to God with signs too deep for words. (Romans 8:26-27 TPT)

These are examples of how we can approach God in prayer for ourselves, as well as asking the Holy Spirit to lead us in our prayers.

1. A daily passion and hunger for God in His Word. (Matthew 4:4)

2. Pray for an obedient heart to hear and apply what you learn from God's Word. (James1:22)
3. A mind of discernment. (Philippians 1:9-10)
4. Knowledge of God's Word daily. (Colossians 1:9-10)
5. To know the love of Christ more deeply. (Ephesians. 3:14,18,19)
6. Hope enriches God's glorious inheritance. (Ephesians 1:18-19)
7. Strength and endurance (Ephesians 3:16)
8. Greater understanding of God's power in me. (Ephesians 6:16; I John 4:4)
9. Ever increasing faith. (Mark 9:24)
10. Do not yield to temptation. (Matthew 6:13)
11. To develop the fruits of the Spirit richly and responsibly. (Galatians 5:22)
12. Boldness to preach the gospel and bear good fruit. (Matthew 28:18)

UTILIZING OUR MOST POWERFUL WEAPON

You have not because you ask not. James.4:2 KJV

8 keys for more prayer power.

Focus is key.

1. Know, to whom you are speaking - "My father" (Matthew 6:9)
2. Thank Him. Our heart of gratitude pleases God. (Psalms 136:1-9)
3. Ask for his will. The safest place we can be is God's will. (Matthew 6:10)
4. Say what you need. Ask God to provide. (Genesis 22:14)

5. Ask for forgiveness. Check your heart. (Matthew 16:12)
6. Pray with a friend in agreement. (Matthew 18:2)
7. Say what God says. The word of God has power in it. It is our great spiritual weapon. (2 Corinthians 10:4-5)
8. Memorizing scripture intimately will add strength and authority to your prayers. (Psalms 119:11-16).

CHAPTER 5

GOD'S PURPOSE FOR ME

WHY DO I EXIST?

I was created for God by Him. All things were created in heaven and on earth. (Colossians 1:16 AMP)

What is God's purpose for me?

Have you ever asked yourself this question?

Truth is, God has never created anything without a purpose. Colossians 1.16 States, everything began in God and finds its purpose in Him.

The very fact that we are alive means God has a purpose for our lives!

If you are searching for your purpose in life, don't worry about seeking out your gifts and talents, your goals or visions. Start with your first and most important purpose, knowing and loving God. Everything else will fall into its place when you seek first to fulfill this purpose in your life. (Matthew 6:33).

We must seek the One who gives us purpose first, our Creator.

He alone is the one who knows why He created us.

The word of God says, "God is love". Love is the essence of his character.

God created us as an object of his love.

We are made to be loved by God.

The only accurate way to understand ourselves is by what God does for us. (I Corinthians 2:9)

God did not need to love us because he wasn't lonely.

He didn't need servants. He wasn't bored. God created us because he wanted to love us. We are planned for His purpose. (Psalms 144:4; Psalms 147:11).

The first purpose for our lives is to know and love God because that gives him pleasure. (Jeremiah 31:3). The most important thing we can do in life is to reciprocate the love He gives God.

Jesus said to love the Lord your God with every passion of your heart. This is the first and greatest commandment, so instead of trying to do and say all the right things to make God love us, all we have to do is realize that He loves us already; so love Him back.

When we love God, we should want to express that love. How to express that love? First, through worship. (Psalms 147; Psalms 95:6-7; John 4:23). Whenever we are singing a song, praying and thanking God in our hearts; that's worship. Worship is simply anything that gives God pleasure and should be the first purpose of our life.

We now know what makes God happy! We should be propelled to pursue these things that please Him, and God will help us in that pursuit. All we need to do is ask, talk to God and He will talk back to us. Prayer is vital to the process of a fulfilled purpose life. (Proverbs 3:6).

Consider this prayer as an example or pray as you are led by the Holy Spirit.

PRAYER

Dear Heavenly Father, if I don't get anything else done today, help me to know you a little bit better and love you a little bit more. Lord Jesus, if at the end of the day if I know you a little bit better and love you a little bit more, I have not wasted this day. If I love you and know you a little bit more, I just fulfill the first purpose of my life in the name of the Lord Jesus, Amen.

PEACE "SHALOM"

You will keep him in perfect peace, whose mind is stayed on you. Isaiah 26:3 ESV

Christ's peace refers to hope and reassurance. Peace is a wonderful gift Jesus left us. He wants us to experience full peace. (John 14:27).

Jesus, you are close to me. I experience your peace when I am crushed in spirit and my heart is broken.

Lord Jesus, your peace is imparted into me. I enjoy peace in my life.

Thank you, Jesus, for giving to me and leaving me with your peace.

Thank you, Lord Jesus, your peace is not like man's peace, or a temporary fix, your piece is eternal.

Lord Jesus, you give me peace in the midst of my storms.

Thank you, Jesus, for giving me a peace that's not fragile, so I am not troubled or afraid.

I will be anxious for nothing because I present my request to God and rest in His peace.

Thank you, Jesus, for giving me peace with God, peace with others, and peace with myself.

I confess I am blessed because I work for peace. I am called a child of God

Lord Jesus, I confess I am fully covered because I embrace your peace.

I release your peace. Oh Lord, I accept your peace. I seek your peace. I engage your peace.

Oh Lord, I confess I have all understanding, my heart and mind are guarded by your peace.

I will not try to figure out my problems. Lord, I will rest in your peace.

I am at peace with my past because Jesus helps me to get passed my past.

Speak Shalom, wholeness, and completeness because Jesus became the complete sacrifice for my sins.

I declare I am a peacemaker.

I will plant seeds of peace and reap the harvest of good things.

I am filled with joy, peace, and believing through the power of the Holy Spirit.

I am thankful I have peace with God and Christ through the blood of Jesus.

Our God be glorified; Our God be praised in the name of Jesus Christ, Amen.

FOCUS ON GOD

Let all that I am praise the Lord; May I never forget the good things He does for me. He forgives all my sins and heals all my diseases. He redeemed me from death and crowns me with love and tender mercies. He fills my life with good things. My youth is renewed like the eagles. Psalms 103:3-5 NLT

I declare I have a focus on God that nothing can change or hinder or destroy.

My faith looks backward to remember and count the many blessings of God so I can gain strength and move ahead.

I will rehearse all God's blessings, often as a source of encouragement and faith each day.

I will meditate on God's thankfulness he never changes. (Hebrews 13:8)

I am assured of God's faithfulness in the future. He's the same always. I declare my mind is set in a forward focus on God, my Helper.

I declare when trouble nears my mind, my heart sets in a forward focus on God.

Faith in God will enable me to be confident in a faithful God who loves me. I will trust my God. For protection and provision. (Psalms 91:9-13)

Whenever anxiety and sorrow show up. I will look to my Lord for my needed comfort. He will never abandon or forsake me. (Psalms 94:19).

Thank you, Jesus. Amen.

THE HEALER IS HERE

He forgives all my sins and heals all my diseases. (Psalms 103:3 ESV)

Lord Jesus, thank you. You forgive all our sins and heal all our diseases. "The Healer is here."

Lord Jesus, thank you for your supernatural power to heal all our sicknesses. "The Healer is here."

Heavenly Father, thank you for your covenant promise for physical healing from diseases and sickness. "The Healer is here."

Thank you, Lord Jesus, for a mind to believe by faith for our healing. "The Healer is here."

Thank you, Lord Jesus, for revealing the will of Father God to heal us. (Matthew 4:23) "The Healer is here."

Oh, Lord, our Redeemer. Thank you. You are a savior and a healer. "The Healer is here."

Thank you, Lord, for the stripes you bore on your body so we could be healed. "The Healer is here."

Thank you, Lord Jesus, for dying for us so we can be healed. "The Healer is here."

Lord Jesus, thank you for your resurrection power, the ultimate sacrifice for a permanent healing. "The Healer is here."

I confess I am forever healed because of your love for me, Lord Jesus. "The Healer is here."

Oh, praise his holy name. "Jesus is here."

WE ARE ALL IN THIS TOGETHER

This is the first and greatest commandment. Love the Lord your God with all your heart, all your soul, and all your mind. A second is equally important: Love your neighbor as yourself. Matthew 22:38-39 NLT

Focus: Christians helping others.

As I look around, I see so much division among Christians. I deal with it on a daily basis only because I believe differently. I am an outcast, often ostracized, and at times ridiculed or slandered. I am proud to be of the oneness doctrine (one God, One Faith, and One Baptism), and I refuse to keep silent as to what the Lord has revealed to me; to be his true and correct word. I also refuse to participate in what I term "Christian sibling rivalry". Nor will I lower myself to arguing among my brethren or slandering their names.

Apostolic, Baptist. Pentecostal, Protestant… the list goes on and on. All claim to be correct in their interpretation of God's Word. Many go as far as to claim that theirs is the only correct way to worship or way to heaven while they point fingers at each other like children. If a person believes in their truth and confesses with their mouth that the Lord Jesus is Lord, that he sacrificed himself for our sins, was resurrected; if they have truly repented of their sins and accepted Christ Jesus as their Savior, then I will call that person my brother or sister.

Honestly, I do not believe that Come Judgment Day, Christ will say you serve me faithfully, you repented of your sins, and you accepted me as your Savior, but you didn't believe in my doctrine of tongues, so I am condemning you to hell. It is man that focuses on the trivial matters of faith or who is holier. Christ taught love, acceptance, and forgiveness.

He taught us to help each other, encourage one another, and not to judge.

Christ tells us to love also our enemies. Christ told us we should love everyone, including sinners who persecute us. He went one step further when it came to loving our brethren. A new commandment I give you to love one another just as I love you.

In Matthew 19:19; 22:39; Mark 12:31 and Luke 10:27 - Christ quotes Leviticus 19:18 Love your neighbor as yourself. Christ also tells us to love our enemies (Matthew 5:44 KJV). In Luke 6:27 Christ told us we should love everyone including sinners who persecute us. He went one step further when it comes to loving our brethren. A new commandment I give to you: love one another just as I love you. John 13:34,15:12 KJV

We are all one body; we are all brothers and sisters, and it falls on us to help one another. Failing to love one another is disobedient to His command. Let us love one another for love is God. God teaches us to love. Christ gave us His example to follow. He showed us what love is; if Christ abides in us that same love abides in us for our brethren. God writes it on our hearts that love and ability to love our brethren with agape love, love with forgiveness, non-judging, all-encompassing sacrificial love is God-given. We are not to condemn our brethren or hold grudges, we are to forgive them and help them all. I Thessalonians 5:14 We are to bear one another's burdens. Galatians 6:2, Those of us that are strong have an obligation to bear the failing of the weak. Romans 15:1 We are not to live selfishly. As mature Christians is up to us to strengthen our brethren to share their burdens with them instead of looking down on our brethren who may be going through trials and having a difficult time enduring. Now more than ever, we must unite and help each other win while the world is watching to see how we will act. In the world we live in today, the effects of wide felt unemployment, alcoholism, depression, suicide and crime rates have all increased. The world is watching to see what Christ's ambassadors on the earth and his living witnesses will do. Will we show them a body divided? A group of uncaring judgmental elitists? Or will we show them Christ through our caring, loving, supporting, strengthening, sacrificial, compassionate acts of love? Christ led by example His commandment to love one another. Let us show the world that we are his disciples, and we are all in this together.

Author: Mr. Timothy Jones

CHAPTER 6

THE GOOD BOOK

This book is laced with God's Word and toxic to the enemy of God's people. God's Word has a deliverance healing effect upon those who speak, sing, pray, and spread His word. I invite you to take a journey through these pages. Let God's Word have an intoxicating positive effect as you eat and drink of the Word of God. The Word of God reveals the true nature of man, life issues, and what we need to change. Life is going to happen with all its problems, but there is an answer. It's in the Word of God. This book offers help in difficult times.

LIVING GOD'S WAY

Uplifting inspirations in faith field encouragement. Building unshakable faith in an age of discouragement.

Watch what God does and then you do it like children who learn proper behavior from their parents. All what God does is love for you. Ephesians 5:1-2 MSG

Help us, O Lord, in everything we do to represent you as your sons and daughters.

Father God, help us to continue to walk, surrender to the extravagant love of Christ. His great love was pleasing to you like an aroma of adoration, a sweet healing fragrance.

Oh Lord, I confess my deeds and character. I mimic yours. I am filled with your thoughts and your love.

Oh Lord, we are your holy ones. We keep ourselves from worthless words that bring disgrace and dishonor to your name.

Bless us, O Lord, with worship words to fill our hearts and overflow, spilling out and manifesting your love.

Oh Lord, I confess I will not be guilty of the impure things that defile your kingdom

I confess I live a life of abundant righteousness through You, Lord Jesus Christ.

I declare I am one big bundle of submitted, committed, obedient, consuming fire to all unrighteousness.

Father God, I am thankful I am living in your love. Your love covers all.

Father, Lord, help us to live our lives your way, so the perfect example of love you require can be seen in us because it's the most effective sermon we will ever preach. Thank you, Jesus, Amen.

SPIRITUAL WARFARE

A final word: Be strong in the Lord and in His mighty power. Put on all of God's armor so that you will be able to stand firm against all strategies of the devil. Ephesians 6:10-18 NLT

There is a war going on. We may not always sense that we are a part of the battle scene. Thank you, Lord Jesus, I am supernaturally infused with strength through my life union with you. I confess Lord Jesus; I stand victorious with the force of Your Holy Ghost power flowing in and through me.

I decree and declare I am protected as I stand against the strategies of the enemy. My weapons are not carnal but mighty to pull down enemy strongholds.

I confess I am armed and dangerous with my key offense weapon of prayer.

I am equipped against the enemy's attack.

I confess I know who I am. I have authority over all the enemy through the blood of Jesus.

I declare I never will kick back and take it easy because there is a real adversary who seeks to destroy my testimony.

I declare and decree my shoulder faith is always up along with the heart of God to withstand the adversaries' assaults in the name of the Lord Jesus, Amen.

THE BATTLE IS THE LORD'S STAY CALM

The Lord himself will fight for you, just stay calm. Exodus 14:14 NLT

Sometimes, Oh Lord, you call us to action.

Sometimes you call us through weeping, prayer, and fasting.

But sometimes you call us to do nothing but be still and trust you in the process.

Father God, when we find ourselves in a place in life when we are not sure what to do, help us to pause and check in with you. Thank you, oh Lord, you are a man of war, and you don't need me to do anything.

Lord Jesus, I wear your whole armor which enables me to stand.

I Declare I will stay calm and obey your command.

Oh Lord, your weapons are indestructible because of your mighty power. We cannot be defeated; we are fighting from Victory.

Thank you, Lord, you have equipped your people to stand against any rival.

Your weapons are sufficient for every stronghold and destruction that lay in our path.

Lord Jesus, you conquered all through your resurrection.

Thank you, Father. Lord, our enemies are defeated by your consuming fire.

I will not fear, because every weapon formed against me will not prosper. I declare all will fail and die.

God will reveal the plans of my enemy to me every time. I will not fear my enemy because I have God-given authority.

I confess I am a winner and not a loser for the battle of my soul, because the battle is not mine, it's the Lord's.

Thank you, oh Lord. The blood of the Lamb and the word of our testimony is our defense to overcome, and it is our sufficiency to get us safely home. Thank you, Jesus. Amen.

MAKE WISE CHOICES, STOP WASTING YOUR TIME

Watch out that you do not lose what you have worked so hard to achieve. Be diligent so that you receive your full reward. 2John 1:8 NLT

Life is brief, we can't afford to waste time. Life is a vapor. Man is frail and we don't have control.

God has a plan. He does not need our permission to act or activate his plan.

Whose plan are we working? Who guides our lives?

Every choice is important and is essential for our future.

Every decision leads us somewhere.

Life is uncertain.

Life is not a problem to be solved. It is a gift to be enjoyed.

This is the day the Lord has made; let us rejoice and be glad in it. (Psalms 118:24) ESV

Do life. If at first you don't succeed, try reading the instructions in the Word.

Take fast hold of instructions. Let her not go. Keep her, for she is thy life. (Proverbs 4:13) KJV

The measure of a man is not how great his faith is, but how great his love is.

Now these three remain-faith, hope, love. But the greatest of these is love. 1 Corinthians 13:13 NIV

Be a good example. People may doubt what you say, but they will always believe what you do. The tree is known and recognized and judged by its fruit. Matthew 12:33

WHAT JESUS SAYS ABOUT LIFE

I am the Way, the truth and the life. No one can come to the Father except through me. John 14:6-7 NIV

1. I have come that you may have life and that it may be more abundant. John 10:10 KJV
2. Jesus said I am the bread of life. John 6:35, 48, 51 ESV
3. I have the words of eternal life. John 6:68-69 ESV
4. Whoever finds me has eternal life. Proverbs 8:35 ESV
5. Whoever believes in me has eternal life. John 11:25-26 ESV
6. Whoever believes in me, his name will be written down in the Lambs Book of Life. Revelation 13:8 ESV

All our questions are answered in one verse, John 14:6. All we need, we find in the Lord Jesus Christ. The gateway of life is narrow, and we need to know how to navigate through life. Jesus is the way. When things are difficult, we need connection for directions. Jesus says to his disciples in John 14:6 NIV, "I am the way".

Thank you, Jesus, for making a way for us. Men today are searching for something that is real and true. We need to hear truth. We can never know the truth of our circumstances unless we know Jesus. We don't always realize where we truly stand in life. That truth has power over all our circumstances. We are searching for something that will last for life; we live to leave a legacy or inheritance. The search for what will last forever. A life that will never end. Look no further, Jesus is life everlasting. John 10:10. This is what it's all about. Our money will perish, our vacation will end, our beauty will fade, but Jesus will never end. It's all in him, the way, the truth, the life, Jesus.

THE BATTLE

He spoke. Listen all you people of Judah and Jerusalem. Listen, King Jehoshaphat! This is what the Lord says: "Do not be afraid, don't be discouraged by this mighty army, for this battle is not yours, but God's." II Chronicles 20:15NLT

Today I pray I received divine strength from you, my Father God.

I will not pray a miss.

I command warring angels of God to descend and fight on my behalf.

As I intercede in war and prayer, I declare my prayer will not be in vain but will bring solution and produce divine intervention.

I seek, I knock, I ask, I decree and declare

I am under an open heaven. I receive the favor and blessings of the Almighty God.

Heaven is moving, earth is shaking, my sovereign God is working.

I shall win and not lose any battles because the Lord is with me.

I declare and decree that I am more than a conqueror through the Lord Jesus Christ.

His love for me and my love for him destroys all my enemies plans to kill, steal and destroy.

I come against and stand on the Word of God.

The enemies looking to destroy me is overcome by the blood of the Lamb and the word of my testimony.

I take captive of every evil thought that tries to hinder me from my Kingdom purpose.

I declare and decree my mind is free and not in captivity to any enemy influences.

I commend every wall barrier, and every mountain to fall flat, and every yoke that burdens be destroyed.

As I have spoken in my prayers, I decree and declare it is done in the name of the Lord Jesus Christ, Amen.

THE GOOD SHEPHERD PSALM 23

The Lord is my best friend and my shepherd.

I always have more than enough.

He offers a resting place for me

In His luxurious love.

His tracks take me to an Oasis of peace

The cry is a pasture of bliss

That's where He restores and revives my life.

He opens before me pathways to God's pleasures and leads me along
in His footsteps of righteousness

So, I can bring honor to His name.

Lord, even when your path takes me through the valley. The deepest
darkness, fear will never conquer me, for you already have.

Your authority is my strength and my peace

The comfort of your love takes away my fear.

I'll never be lonely. You are near.

You become my delicious feast, even when my enemies dare to fight,
you anoint me with the fragrance of your Holy Spirit. You give me
all I can drink of you until my heart overflows.

So why would I fear the future?

For your goodness and love, pursue me all the days of my life.

Then afterwards, when my life is through, I'll return to your glorious
presence to be with you forever. Psalm 23

VICTORY IN JESUS

When the perishable puts on the imperishable, and the mortal put on immortality, then shall come to pass the saying that it is written, death is swallowed up in victory. Oh death, where is your victory? Oh death, where is your sting? I Corinthians 15:54-55 ESV

Glory, glory, hallelujah, since I laid my burdens down.

Lord Jesus, it's in you where my victory is found.

Through many dangers in this life, I have already come.

My mind looks back in awesome wonder where you have brought me from.

You delivered me out of darkness into your marvelous life.

When everything was going wrong, you made everything alright. When my enemies come against me to kill, steal and destroy, my prayer, praise and worship showed up and you won for me, the war

I confess there is none like you, Lord Jesus, who is so faithful and so true.

The battle in this life is never mine, that's a job for you.

So, I stand aside. My Lord and Savior, I would not get in your way.

You triumph over every enemy that's standing come what may.

Will not escape your destroying power. Not any day

Hallelujah, Our God be praised. Amen.

WHO IS LIKE YOU LORD?

On his robe is written this title: King Of kings and Lord of all Lords. Revelation 19:16 NLT

Praise the Lord!
For the Lord our God, the Almighty reigns. Revelation 19:6B NLT
All glory and honor, salvation and adoration all belong to you
Nothing in this universe can ever be so true.
You are the way, the truth and the life
Where you always deliver from pain, misery and strife.
You, oh Lord, are present in all my tomorrow's
You have prepared a place for me to escape every sorrow.
I put my trust in you, Lord Jesus, so I won't have to fight
You are my security that makes everything alright.
My enemies cannot stand in the presence of your holy power
They will surely perish, run, hide and cover.
I give all praise to you, my Lord and Majesty
That our enemies and our foes are now a casualty.
Who is like you, O Lord in your magnificent glory
Those who tried to defeat you never live to tell the story.
Your power is the greatest that none other can succeed
It produces every necessity that man will ever need.
Thank you, Jesus. Amen.

A SHOUT WITH CLOUT

A Jericho. Prayer.

So, the people shouted, when the priest blew with the trumpets: and it came to pass, when the people heard the sound of the trumpet, and the people shouted with a great shout that the walls fell down flat so that the people went into the city. Every man's straight before him and they took the city. Joshua 6:20 KJV

No need to worry, you will have the same results, in your life now, as it was for Joshua and the saints back then.

You have the clout. It's in your shout. Make your shout count, say something.

This prayer was given by inspiration of the Almighty God to my daughter, Dewana Allen. It is a victory prayer that will help us to ascend to a higher level of living as we focus our attention on what's required of us to accomplish God's will and assignment in our lives.

THE JERICHO PRAYER

To our gracious and loving God, Heavenly Father, King of Kings and Lord of Lords, I glorify your name. To lift my voice, focus, and praise you for awesome power and eternal victory. Lord, you are God Almighty the one that defeats every enemy and brings down every wall

Father, I honor You for your unshakable authority and dominion over all things

Lord, I come before you, humbly placing every wall, barrier, and challenge that I face at your feet. In the name of Jesus, I declare that victory is assured over all spiritual warfare that seeks to hinder my progress and keep me from my breakthrough.

I rebuke every spirit of confusion, unbelief, and discouragement that may try to stand against me In Jesus name. Lord, I declare freedom from lack, obstacles, disappointments, dry valleys, stagnation, and everything that gets in the way of growth and blessings in my life.

Lord, you know every detail, every barrier and chain that's been holding me back. in the name of Jesus, I pray that these obstacles be removed.

That the dry spell comes to an end and the stagnation will cease.

I reject every negative word spoken over my life to prevent me from receiving the blessings you have for me and I come against anything that is not of you Jesus. in Jesus name I rebuke anything that is keeping me from moving forward and your purpose and plan for my life.

I ask for your forgiveness and tender mercies this day. My love for you is forever Jesus.

Almighty God, I believe in your power to change my circumstances, to bring life where there is barrenness, to open doors where there have been walls.

Let your living waters flow in the dry areas of my life and renew me with fresh strength and vitality.

Lord, I come against any form of delay or resistance that the enemy may be placing in my way, I declare victory over it in Jesus' name.

I trust that you God will guide me past the obstacles and into the fruitful season that you have prepared for me.

Father, I ask that your blessings overflow in my life.

Let your favor surround me and open doors that no man can shut. I declare in the name of Jesus that blessing and abundance are my portion in Jesus' name. May your healing touch be over every area of my life.

Restore my body, mind and soul and make me whole.

I rebuke every sickness, disease and infirmity in my life. in Jesus' name I pray a hedge of protection around me and keep me from all harm and evil.

I declare in the name of Jesus that no weapon formed against me shall prosper and I will dwell in safety under your wings.

Father, I declare in Jesus name that every chain will break, and every barrier will fall.

I trust in your promises, and I believe that your timing is perfect.

Fill me with your unwavering faith and guide me on the path to victory.

I thank you in advance for my up-and-coming breakthrough.

Father, with you I know that all things are possible.

I believe that all walls and barriers in my life will come down Just like the walls of Jericho.

Heavenly Father, I pray that you will increase my faith that I may believe without wavering in your unchanging love.

Help me to see beyond my circumstances and focus on Your eternal truths. Strengthen my trust in You Lord, that I may walk in confidence knowing that you are in control of every situation and your timing is perfect.

Lord, remove any doubt, fear or unbelief from me. May you replace it with a strong, steadfast faith that can move mountains and can tear down walls that have been holding me back

Thank you, merciful, loving God, for hearing my prayer in the mighty name of the Lord Jesus Christ, Amen.

PRAYER

Heavenly Father. Almighty God, Creator of heaven and Earth, I come to the throne of grace with thanksgiving and reverence. Your power is beyond comprehension. Your love and mercy are endless. You are the Alpha and the Omega, the beginning and the end, the author and finisher of our faith.

I stand in awe of your majesty and splendor, humbled and overwhelmed by your grace.

Lord, I thank you for the freedom you have given me through your Son, Jesus Christ.

I'm grateful for the chains you have broken, the prison doors you have opened, and the new life you have breathed into me.

Thank you for seeing me not as I was, but who I am.

Merciful Father, I ask for Your forgiveness for my sins and the times I have lived beneath my true identity in You. Forgive me for the moments I have allowed fear, doubt, and insecurity to hold me back.

As you have forgiven me, I also forgive those who have wronged me.

Releasing all anger and bitterness. In the name of Jesus, I declare and decree that I'm loose from every bondage.

I rebuke every spirit of fear, doubt, and unworthiness. In the name of Jesus, I bind the lies of the enemy that have kept me captive, and I claim the truth of your word that every generational curse, every ungodly soul tie, and every stronghold that have held me back is broken.

Father, I pray for deeper revelation of my true identity in Christ.

Open the eyes of my heart to see myself as you see me; help me to embrace the truth that I am your beloved child, chosen and set apart for your purposes. In the strong name of the Lord Jesus, Amen.

CHAPTER 7

UNSHAKEABLE WINNING FAITH

THE GOOD FIGHT OF FAITH

Fight the good fight of faith, lay hold of eternal life, where unto thou art also called, and host professed a good profession before many witnesses. I Timoth 6:12 NKJV

I will continually fight to believe God's word

Because the enemy will try to steal the word from me.

Thoughts and unbelief and doubt are not my candidates

I fight to hold on to what I believe.

I feed on God's word until it is strong in me

Nothing can move me from it, and no one can talk me out of it.

I see myself with the manifestation of completion as the last words in my life.

I see it with my spiritual eyes as done.

I am fully persuaded that what God promised, He is able to do. Romans 4:21

I continually fight the good fight of faith, saying what the word of God says.

I will never face my enemies, trials or problems with my mouth shut.

Believing and saying is not my idea but God's pattern. Hebrews 11:3

Lord, I confess I'm created in your likeness, and I imitate you. Genesis 1:3-28; Genesis 1:26; Ephesians 5:1

Lord Jesus, help us to pray exactly what you say in your word

Because it's then when I am lifted out of defeat and set on the path to victory.

Father, Lord, when I speak your words in faith, it strengthens my spirit and renews my mind and gives me a positive attitude.

Lord Jesus, help me to use your God-given authority, Your name and Your Word over all the power of the enemy.

I resist the enemy, and he runs from me.

I confess, "In Christ, I am a winner."

And I act victoriously because that's how God sees me. Thank you, Jesus. Amen.

STAY ALIVE

Afterward He ate some food and regained his strength. Acts 9:19 NLT

Draw us out of our dead place, Lord.

I declare your power of life is moving in our place.

Fulfill the need in me to learn how to embrace change.

Change my mind more to embrace things that will impact my tomorrows into success.

Help me to make decisions that's going to impact my life and the lives of others.

Change can be challenging, but help me Lord to have a mind of positive ideas

Or help me to have an ascended mind

So, I can rise to a higher level of thinking.

I confess everything is going up from here

I declare I have an external awareness of Kingdom thought and the things that are above.

I have Kingdom authority and Lord; you want me to use it demonstrating your love.

Father God, help me to use the potential you have put in me to advance your Kingdom on earth.

Help me to see that the Holy Spirit in me is not just to shout, dance, and speak in tongues.

Lord Jesus, shift my thinking to Kingdom thinking no matter what may come.

I do not limit myself to less than what God called me to be.

I think of myself like God thinks of me and what he did to set me free.

Whatever I must do, I will stay alive, stay committed to do what God's will is for me.

In the strong name of the Lord Jesus. Amen.

THE BODY GUARD (A PROMISE FROM GOD)

But in the coming days, no weapon turned against you will succeed. You will silence every voice raised up to accuse you. Those benefits are enjoyed by the servants of the Lord. Isaiah 54:17 NLT

God is building us and nothing God builds can ever be destroyed.

Peace and security are in our God.

He is our bodyguard.

God says if people get together and try to attack us, he will fight for us.

If we are serving God and walking in his ways, we can expect God to protect and defend us. He is our bodyguard.

Where people try to tear us down in words and actions, God promises to fight for us. He gives us a good name. We have our Father's DNA. Made in His image. Know who you are in Him.

Lord, you are our bodyguard.

Thank you, Lord, for your consistent presence in a world of chaos, sadness, and instabilities.

Lord, you are the bodyguard.

Thank you, God Jehovah, for providing your steadfast, consistent love we can rely on. You are our bodyguard.

Your power will never fade away. Your power is far greater than the enemy's.

You are our bodyguard.

Thank you, Jesus, your church will not be destroyed. You are our bodyguard.

Father God in all your awesome, potent power, you will protect your church, the body of Christ.

I declare and decree whatever weapon is raised against God's people. Is in danger of being destroyed.

I declare anyone looking to do evil against your people, Lord Jesus cause it to fail. Ephesians 6:13, Romans 8:38-39.

You are our bodyguard.

PRAYER

Lord God Almighty, thank you for giving us your guidance, protection and strength.

Thank you for your promise to be our bodyguard.

Thank you, Heavenly Father, you will never abandon us.

Oh Lord, thank you for being faithful to always be our eternal Redeemer who protects the church, "Christ's body."

You are our bodyguard. I will love you forever. All praise and glory and honor be to you, our great Savior and Lord. Amen.

VICTORY IN JESUS (SONG)

This song speaks of the redeeming power of Jesus from start to finish. (1John 5:4)

This is an overcoming winning song. Everyone born of God has overcome the world.

I heard an old, old story
How a savior came from glory,
How he gave his life on Calvary to save a wretch like me,
I heard about his groaning of his precious blood atoning,
Then I repented of my sins
And won the victory. Oh, victory in Jesus my Savior forever
He sought me and brought me with his redeeming blood
He loved me ere I knew him and all my love is due him,
He plunged me to victory beneath the cleansing flood.
I heard about his healing of his cleansing power revealing.

How he made the lane to walk again
And caused the blind to see.
And then I cried, "Dear Jesus"
Come here, my broken spirit.
And somehow Jesus came and brought me to victory.
Author Eugene M Bartlett.

SCRIPTURES OF ASCENDED LIFE

John 1:51 (ESV)
And he said to him, "Truly, truly, I say to you, you will see heaven opened, and the angels of god ascending and descending on the Son of Man."

1 Peter 3:22 (ESV)
Who has gone into heaven and is at the right hand of God, with angels, authorities, and powers having been subjected to him.

John 1:1-51 (ESV)
In the beginning was the Word, and the Word was with God, and the Word was God. He was in the beginning with God. All things were made through him, and without Him was not anything made that was made. In Him was life, and the life was the light of men. The light shines in the darkness, and the darkness has not overcome it...

Hebrews 1:14 (ESV)
Are they not all ministering spirits sent out to serve for the sake of those who are to inherit salvation?

Romans 8:34 (ESV)

Who is to condemn? Christ Jesus is the one who died-more than that, who was raised-who is at the right hand of God, who indeed is interceding for us.

John 3:16 (ESV)
"For God so loved the world, that he gave his only Son, that whoever believes in him should not perish but have eternal life.

Matthew 3:16 (ESV)
And when Jesus was baptized, immediately he went up from the water, and behold, the heavens were opened to him, and he saw the Spirit of God descending like a dove and coming to rest on him.

Psalm 24:7 (ESV)
Life up your heads, O gates! And be lifted up, O ancient doors, that the King of glory may come in.

3 John 1:4 (ESV)
I have no greater joy than to hear that my children are walking in the truth.

Hebrews 3:6 (ESV)
But Christ is faithful over God's house as a son. And we are his house, if indeed we hold fast our confidence and our boasting in our hope.

1Timothy 2:5(ESV)
For there is one God, and there is one mediator between God and men, the man Christ Jesus.

Ephesians 4:7-8(ESV)
But grace was given to each one of us according to the measure of Christ's gift. Therefore it says, "when he ascended on high he led a host of captives, and he gave gifts to men."

John 16:28 (ESV)
I came from the Father and have come into the world, and now I am leaving the world and going to the Father."

Matthew 16:18(ESV)
And I tell you, you are Peter, and on this rock, I will build my church, and the gates of hell shall not prevail against it.

Genesis 28:15 (ESV)
Behold, I am with you and will keep you wherever you go and will bring you back to this land. For I will not leave you until I have done what I have promised you"

Printed in the United States
by Baker & Taylor Publisher Services